Save the Pandas

THIS EDITION
Editorial Management by Oriel Square
Produced for DK by WonderLab Group LLC
Jennifer Emmett, Erica Green, Kate Hale, *Founders*

Editors Grace Hill Smith, Libby Romero, Maya Myers Michaela Weglinski;
Photography Editors Kelley Miller, Annette Kiesow, Nicole DiMella;
Managing Editor Rachel Houghton; **Designers** Project Design Company;
Researcher Michelle Harris; **Copy Editor** Lori Merritt; **Indexer** Connie Binder;
Proofreader Larry Shea; **Reading Specialist** Dr. Jennifer Albro; **Curriculum Specialist** Elaine Larson

---

Published in the United States by DK Publishing
1745 Broadway, 20th Floor, New York, NY 10019

Copyright © 2023 Dorling Kindersley Limited
DK, a Division of Penguin Random House LLC
23 24 25 26 10 9 8 7 6 5 4 3 2 1
001-334106-Oct/2023

All rights reserved.

Without limiting the rights under the copyright reserved above, no part of this publication may be reproduced, stored in or introduced into a retrieval system, or transmitted, in any form, or by any means (electronic, mechanical, photocopying, recording, or otherwise), without the prior written permission of the copyright owner.
Published in Great Britain by Dorling Kindersley Limited

A catalog record for this book
is available from the Library of Congress.
HC ISBN: 978-0-7440-7492-5
PB ISBN: 978-0-7440-7493-2

DK books are available at special discounts when purchased in bulk for sales promotions, premiums, fundraising, or educational use. For details, contact: DK Publishing Special Markets,
1745 Broadway, 20th Floor, New York, NY 10019
SpecialSales@dk.com

Printed and bound in China

The publisher would like to thank the following for their kind permission to reproduce their images:
a=above; c=center; b=below; l=left; r=right; t=top; b/g=background

Alamy Stock Photo: Benoit Douchez / Pairi Daiza / Abacapress.com 16, Arterra Picture Library / Clement Philippe 24-25, David Leadbitter 20bl, Cyril Ruoso / Minden Pictures 18crb, Katherine Feng / Minden Pictures 17cl, 17br, Mitsuaki Iwago / Minden Pictures 27br, ZSSD / Minden Pictures 26bl, SCPhotos / Dallas, John Heaton 4-5; **Dreamstime.com:** Galinasavina 8ca, Hungchungchih 28-29, Isselee 18bl, 30cla, Gueret Pascale 12bl, Plej92 20-21, Slowmotiongli 8-9, Kenny Tong 18-19, Tulipmix 3; **Fotolia:** Eric Isselee 1; **Getty Images:** 500Px Plus / Fernn Quetequitenloviajao 26-27, 30clb, China Photos / Stringer 22-23, 30bl, fStop / Sean Russell 10-11, Moment / © Philippe Lejeanvre 14-15, Stone / Peter Adams 12-13; **naturepl.com:** Gavin Maxwell 10bl, 14bl, 30cl; **Shutterstock.com:** Hung Chung Chih 26br

All other images © Dorling Kindersley
For more information see: www.dkimages.com

For the curious
www.dk.com

Level 1

Save the Pandas

Ruth A. Musgrave

Contents

6	Meet the Panda
10	Scent Trail
12	What's for Lunch?
14	The Best Nest
16	A Baby Is Born

20	Bamboo Bears
22	Working Together
30	Glossary
31	Index
32	Quiz

Meet the Panda

Wild pandas live in only one place on Earth. They live in China, in bamboo forests.

panda

Pandas are bears.
They have paws, claws,
and a short tail.

bamboo

It is cold where pandas live. Thick fur keeps the bears warm.

claws

tail

The black fur might help them hide in shadows. The white fur could make the bears harder to see in the snow.

fur

paw

Scent Trail

Sniff. Rub. Scratch.
The bear sniffs the air, the ground, and a tree. It scratches the tree with its claws.
That lets other bears know it was there.

10

Pandas also use smells to learn about other bears nearby.

What's for Lunch?

The panda sits on the ground to eat.
It holds bamboo with its paws.
Crunch. It munches on the bamboo.

The panda uses its strong teeth and jaws to eat.

The Best Nest

The panda explores. She looks for a den to have her baby. A fallen tree or rocky

nest

cave will work.
The panda makes her nest inside.
The den will keep the mom and baby warm.

A Baby Is Born

The new mom holds her baby. The mother is big. The baby is small.

The cub is safe
and warm with her.
The baby gets milk
from its mother.

Step, step, fall.
The cub takes its
first steps.
It is shaky on its paws.
The baby quickly
learns to climb over
rocks and logs.

Soon, the growing cub races up trees, too. That is a good place to hide while its mom is busy eating.

Bamboo Bears

Pandas need bamboo forests. They cannot live without them. Most bamboo forests are gone.

People cut them down to build roads, towns, and farms.

Working Together

Let's save the pandas! Scientists and other people who love pandas work together. They try to learn more about these bears. They study pandas in the wild and at zoos. People are working to save bamboo forests, too.

The panda sits in the sun.
He looks so cute!
People laugh.
Some zoo visitors watch from just a few feet away.
Others watch on webcams from their homes.
They fall in love with the panda.
They want to protect the bears.

The number of panda bears is getting bigger and bigger. But wild pandas still need help. Their forests will always need protecting.

Today, scientists know a lot about what pandas need to survive.
But they will keep learning more.

The world is coming together to save pandas and bamboo forests.

Glossary

bamboo
a kind of grass that grows into tall trees

cub
a baby bear

den
a nest built inside a log or cave

forest
a place where many trees grow and create homes for animals

scientist
a person who studies animals or other things on Earth

Index

baby   14, 16, 17, 18

bamboo   6, 7, 12, 20, 22, 29

China   6

claws   7, 8, 10

cub   17, 18, 19

den   14

eat   12, 13

forests   6, 20, 22, 26, 28

fur   8, 9

jaws   13

milk   17

nest   14, 15

paws   7, 9, 12, 18

scent trail   10

scientists   22, 28

smells   10, 11

snow   9

tail   7, 8

teeth   13

zoos   22, 24

Quiz

Answer the questions to see what you have learned. Check your answers with an adult.

1. Where do pandas live?
2. What keeps a panda warm?
3. Where do mother pandas make their dens?
4. What do baby pandas eat?
5. True or False: Only scientists can help save pandas.

1. In China, in bamboo forests 2. Fur 3. In fallen trees and rocky caves 4. Milk from their mother 5. False